THIS IS
A BOOK FOR
PEOPLE
WHO LOVE
Birds

DANIELLE BELLENY

Illustrated by Stephanie Singleton

RUNNING PRESS
PHILADELPHIA

Running Press
Hachette Book Group
1290 Avenue of the Americas, New York, NY 10104
www.runningpress.com
@Running_Press

Printed in China

First Edition: April 2022

Published by Running Press, an imprint of Perseus Books, LLC, a
subsidiary of Hachette Book Group, Inc. The Running Press name
and logo is a trademark of the Hachette Book Group.

The Hachette Speakers Bureau provides a wide range of
authors for speaking events. To find out more, go to
www.hachettespeakersbureau.com or call (866) 376-6591.

The publisher is not responsible for websites (or their content) that
are not owned by the publisher.

Text by Danielle Belleny.
Print book cover and interior design by Jenna McBride.

Library of Congress Control Number: 2021949318

ISBNs: 978-0-7624-7597-1 (hardcover), 978-0-7624-7600-8 (ebook)

RRD-S

10 9 8 7 6 5 4 3 2 1

This book is dedicated to my grandparents, Charles and Elizabeth Burse, who showed a young me the wonders of nature.

And to all Black kids who have an endless fascination with nature: Always follow your passions.

Contents

INTRODUCTION:
How the World Got Birds
1

HOW DO BIRDS...
4

BIRD BODIES
16

WATCHING BIRDS
19

**SELECTED BIRDS
OF NORTH AMERICA**
33

Introduction

HOW THE WORLD GOT BIRDS

L et's start with some great news. If you thought you were 65 million years too late to experience dinosaurs, think again. Dinosaurs still walk among us. So where are they? Surprisingly, many—possibly even most—people encounter them daily, and not as lizards, as you might think. Instead, these modern-day dinosaurs come to you and me as birds. Astonishing, yes—but it's all part of an evolutionary plot twist we will discuss shortly. The dinosaur offspring we know today take to the skies with unprecedented flair and fashion, so we can only expect similarly remarkable appearances and behaviors from their ancient relatives. Let's dive a little deeper as we get to know these fascinating creatures all around us.

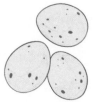

WHAT ARE BIRDS?

About 270 million years ago (mya) lizards and dinosaurs had a common ancestor. The creatures that would evolve into the lizard lineage walked with legs sprawled and bellies to the ground. Their descendants became turtles, snakes, and even more lizards. The dinosaur lineage went on to become theropods— dinosaurs characterized by hollow bones, a wishbone, and a distinctly upright posture. Theropods first appeared 231 mya and ruled the world through terror. As the only carnivorous land animals, theropods bullied their way to the top of the food chain. Their roster included the famous names like *Tyrannosaurus*, *Velociraptor*, *Spinosaurus*, and other terrifying, flesh-eating beasts. Dinosaurs ruled Earth for 160 million years, but 65 mya they were dethroned—swept away along with 75 percent of all life—in one fell swoop by a meteor. All non-avian dinosaurs were extinguished, and from the ashes of those fallen creatures arose the ancestors of modern birds. We can thank one of the world's most catastrophic events for creating a land where today 18,000 species of birds live alongside us.

ANCIENT BIRDS

The progression from dinosaur to bird can be traced to *Archaeopteryx lithographica*, one of the earliest uncovered bird fossils. Undeniably both dinosaur-like and birdlike, the raven-sized *Archaeopteryx lithographica* provides evidence of the pivotal transition from dinosaurs to modern birds 150 mya, including the evolution of feathered wings that supported powered flight.

The birds we encounter today are mere shadows of those of millennia past. In earlier times, you might encounter Terror birds (*Phorusrhacidae*), agile predators with pickaxes for beaks. The joints in their rock-hard skulls were fused together, and their beaks were strong enough to pummel their prey to death. These fearsome creatures used the meat cleaver attached to their faces to tenderize the day's menu items into tearable pieces. One of the largest Terror birds, *Titanis*,  lived in North America, where it spent its days ripping apart mammals until its frightening domination ended about 2.5 mya.

HOW DO BIRDS...

Birds seem to be infinitely influenced by secret signals humans can't perceive. Because of these unseen forces, it can be easy to fall into a string of conspiracy theories about what birds "really" are if you're not careful. Fortunately, there are a lot of *actual* qualities, behaviors, and signals that birds use that are just as cool as the fanciful stories and myths.

SING

If there's one thing birds have, it's range. Songbirds are particularly special because of their ability to learn tunes and perform. Other kinds of birds still use their voices and make simpler sounds that are instinctual rather than learned. The physiology that allows birds to sing more notes than a piano is very unique. Birds have a double-sided voice box, called the *syrinx*, situated where the windpipe branches off to their lungs. To think of this in terms of human anatomy, imagine if your vocal cords were located in your chest instead of at the top of your throat in your larynx. Think of all that extra space! So with birds the process of producing sound can be more involved and offers more diversity. As air passes through the syrinx, it vibrates and creates sound. The two sides of the syrinx can then be individually controlled, which allows birds to sing two different notes simultaneously. Some birds can sing serenades for minutes on end, due in part to the way they take in air. They are really efficient breathers, able to circulate oxygen while both breathing in *and* breathing out. But humans aren't always at a loss to our feathered friends. Their circular breathing strategy is still no match for world-renowned saxophonist Kenny G, who sustained a single sultry note for over 45 minutes.

Birds learn to sing the songs of their kin early in life. Much like human babies, young birds have brains that are very good at picking up language. Young birds must also practice their songs and work up to mastery. Just as human babies babble wet syllables that eventually become their ABCs, young birds will listen to older birds sing, then attempt to copy the older birds' compositions. Practice songs are slightly wonky and a little offbeat at first, but get better with time and tutoring from older birds.

Traditionally, when you hear a North American bird singing, you might assume that it is a male. Males sing their hearts out to attract females and defend their territories. However, depending on the species, both male and female birds can sing complex songs. (And in the tropics, it's common for both sexes to sing all year long.) Female Northern Cardinals, orioles, grackles, and others are known to sing a repertoire of beautifully composed notes. Scientists think it's likely that for millions of years the female ancestors of all modern birds also sang. Overall, the songs of female birds have been severely understudied because of the discipline's bias toward male birdsong. Understanding and researching female birdsong will help unlock important evolutionary questions. And you can be a part of it: contribute your female birdsong observations to online audio libraries to help improve science!

GROW UP

Bird nests fall into three categories: well-built, poorly built, and not built. For well-built nests, look to the Monk Parakeet (*Myiopsitta monachus*) and their downtown apartment–esque nests. These little green birds, also known as Quaker Parrots, live in large communal nests that can be nestled anywhere from trees to utility poles. Their fortresses are multilevel and multi-entry, with a woven ball construction comprised of thorny twigs. All individuals, including the young, spend a tremendous amount of effort on the upkeep of their nests year-round.

Birds can also construct poorly built nests, as the White-winged Dove (*Zenaida asiatica*) does. Dove nests—if  that's what their flimsy piles of twigs can be called—look structurally unsound. Doves also put their nests in questionable places. Prime real estate often includes window ledges and neglected terracotta pots. Despite this low-effort approach to nest building, White-winged Doves are quite prolific and successfully raise juicy babies in their ramshackle homes.

But who said birds have to build nests? Why should a bird waste its talents on building a nest when they can practice sorcery, like Hawaii's Manu-o-Kū (also known as White Terns)? White Terns do not build nests, instead choosing to lay their solo egg on any substrate on which it can be precariously balanced—commonly on a bare branch or rock ledge. Scientists think the White Terns developed this nest-free strategy to avoid parasites. Or maybe White Terns are powerful members of the occult and simply passing down familial traditions to the next generation.

Many baby birds have a distinctive look, which is, in many ways, a lot like octogenarian Vermont senator Bernie Sanders. *Altricial* baby birds tend to look just like furrow-browed old men (of which Sanders is certainly one). Altricial birds are the ones typically born in arboreal nests, or nests high above the ground. Being born high up in a tree is one form of defense against getting eaten by predators, something that is especially necessary as these are some of the most uncoordinated baby birds. They hatch featherless, with closed eyes, and in need of constant care until they leave the nest. The little fleshy nuggets are the perfect size to be after-school snacks for every carnivore around. They'll need all the help they can get to make it out the nest, including a prime perch far away from the ground and its inhabitants.

On the other end of the spectrum are *precocial* baby birds. Any baby bird that runs around like a silly cotton ball with legs is a precocial bird. They hatch feathered and ready to leave the nest, explore the world, and feed themselves. There are even birds called *superprecocial*, and they are *really super.* Some superprecocial species are able to fly the very same day they hatch.

Most bird species do not live in nests year-round. The nest is usually a good place to settle down and be a family bird for a few weeks out of the year. After the young have let their fully formed wings find purchase among the four winds, birds leave the nest to prepare for migration. Once it comes time to hit the road, it's back to finding a safe tree to roost in for the night.

SEE

Overall, birds have excellent vision. Their eyes are relatively large compared to the size of their heads, allowing them a better sense of vision. Having good vision is especially useful when birds are constantly flying between and maneuvering around objects.

Human eyes have three kinds of photoreceptors, which absorb red, blue, and green light. Avian eyes possess the same red, blue, and green photoreceptors, but have 12 times the overall number that humans do, granting them better color vision. Birds also have receptors that give them access to a secret world within the ultraviolet (UV) light spectrum. Birds can use their UV light receptors for everyday tasks like deciding what food is ready to eat and identifying which bird from the flock is their mate. While feathers are already flashy and colorful to our eyes, bird feathers viewed under UV light show that they are always covertly covered in rave paint. The everyday feral pigeon looks quite ordinary to us, but its plain gray wings will show fluorescent pink streaks in the UV spectrum. Male birds of some species will even play with the natural lighting at their breeding grounds by choosing sunny spots to flawlessly display those ultraviolet angles for eligible females.

NAVIGATE

Birds are equipped with the innate skill of knowing where to go and how to get there. Their special ability has been studied by humans for centuries, notably with homing pigeons. Homing pigeons are famous for their ability to find their way home, even when released hundreds of miles away. How do they do it?

During the day, birds can use the position of the sun to navigate, adjusting their flight direction as the sun moves across the sky. At night, birds use the positions of constellations to determine their direction. More impressively, avian species can detect the Earth's magnetic field and employ it as a compass. Magnetic fields are created 1,975 miles (3,178 km) below the Earth's surface, within the planet's liquid outer core. This layer is full of melted metal, which generates electric currents animals can sense. This is just the beginning of understanding bird navigation—and it already sounds fake. Isn't it exciting to live in this absurd world?

It is suspected that birds have special proteins in their eyes, called *cryptochromes*, that can detect the Earth's magnetic field. To put it simply, birds casually use quantum physics to go about their daily lives. Scientists hypothesize that when light enters bird retinas it triggers a series of subatomic events, far outside the scope of this book to explain, to create conditions inside the eye that allow the detection of Earth's magnetic field. What would require humans a slew of specialized high-tech equipment innately takes place inside the wet eyeball of a bird.

Birds are amazing navigators, but even they can still get lost. Some birds do end up way off track and arrive in a foreign country. In 2018, a lone Great Black Hawk, typically found from Mexico to Argentina, was famously documented departing from Texas in April and arriving in Maine by August. The Great Black Hawk made it just in time to see the fall foliage, but this tropical bird was not equipped to withstand sweater weather. To the dismay of thousands of admirers, the Great Black Hawk died from weather-related injuries inflicted by the bone-chilling Maine winter in January 2019. The wayward hawk lives on forever in our hearts, and as a commemorative statue in Portland, Maine, erected below its former perching tree in Deering Oaks Park.

MIGRATE

As the position of the sun changes and daylight begins to wane, a bird's natural urges to move to a sunnier locale are triggered. Many bird species travel between seasons in response to the availability of resources—namely food and nesting sites—participating in a phenomenon called migration. Waterfowl, songbirds, raptors, ducks, and more will travel south in the fall and north in the spring. Migrations are particularly spectacular events because of the extreme distances many birds travel. Before leaving for their vacation homes, birds need to bulk up to ensure they have the energy to complete the trip. Two to three weeks before their expedition, migrant birds will eat enough to double their weight, storing their spare baggage in fat deposits under the skin. Most birds do not complete their migration in one continuous flight. Instead, they will stop over in several places along their route to rest and refuel. A stopover location could be anywhere from a tree in your neighborhood to a state park. Planting shrubs and flowers that are beneficial to wildlife is a great way to help a feathered friend make its way home safely.

Many birds will travel along ancient sky highways to journey from their breeding grounds to their wintering grounds. These pathways, called migratory flyways, provide stepping-stones of habitats with food and shelter along the route. The Americas offer birds in the Western Hemisphere four routes to choose from: the Pacific Flyway, Central Flyway, Mississippi Flyway, and Atlantic Flyway.

BIRD
BODIES

Birds are distinctive in their anatomy, with skeletons and other features that allow them to fly. Let's look at two of the most fascinating features of our avian friends: feathers and bones.

FEATHERS

Let's start on the outside. Most notable are a bird's feathers, which help them regulate body temperature, find a mate, fly, and camouflage. Feathers are made from keratin, just like human hair and nails. You may notice that feathers seemingly cover 99 percent of a bird. However, feathers are arranged in neat tracks that only occur in certain areas of the bird's skin. Just like hairs on a mammal's skin, feathers grow from organized masses of dead proteins that are slowly pushed out from living skin tissue. Beautiful. There are several different kinds of feathers that all serve unique purposes.

If you want to get in-depth knowledge of external bird anatomy, consider researching the "topography of birds." Bird bodies are like a foreign geographic region. The many hills and valleys on a bird's body have specific names that aid in identifying species. When trying to identify especially tricky birds (looking at you, sparrows!), knowing the names and locations of these bird-ographic regions can be helpful.

BONES

Due to the physical demands of flight, avian skeletons are only made up of the bones that are absolutely necessary. A large portion of the bones they do have are fused together, providing strength and the rigidity needed to be airborne. Many people believe birds' knees bend in the opposite direction of our own, but that is not the case. Their fake knees are actually their ankles. Above their ankles, where the fake thighs would be, is their shin and hidden closest to the body underneath feathers are their thighs.

The rumor that bird bones are hollow is true! Well, mostly. Bird bones are not entirely hollow like a straw—they have spongy bone support beams throughout—but there is a considerable amount of open space within them. These open pockets are air sacs that help move oxygen around their body.

WATCHING BIRDS

A NOTE ON THE COMPLICATED HISTORY OF BIRDING

For millennia, cultures around the world have used birds for food, entertainment, navigation, and inspiration. More recently, people en masse have started observing wild birds for recreation and even as a profession. Birding, a cooler name for the hobby known as bird-watching, is the act of enjoying birds for their aesthetics and sounds. A group of white men has often been credited with "pioneering" birding in the 18th century, but  this book isn't going to give crusty dead men the sole credit for creating a hobby that simply seeks to enjoy birds. The beauty of birds has always been recognized.

Birding and ornithology have a group of avian aficionados listed as "founders" of the topics. That list is not only limited in its understanding of ways of knowing; it also includes racists, enslavers, and otherwise problematic white men. For those familiar with the history of North America, it shouldn't come as a surprise that white men took credit for discovering knowledge likely stolen from exploited Indigenous communities. Racism has tarnished everything. Yes, even birds.

The hurdles for underrepresented groups to be involved in birding and the study of birds do not stop there. Many people fall within multiple groups, and their identities have complex intersections. They are met with ableism, sexism, homophobia, gender discrimination, and more just because they want to enjoy birds. What can you expect when the hobby gatekeepers are established, older, rich white men? Racism is so deeply embedded in birding that some birds have even been named after slurs. Birds deserve names that are free from the baggage of socially unacceptable actions. The movement #BirdNamesForBirds, founded by Jordan Rutter and Gabriel Foley, highlights bird species with eponymic and prejudicial names, explains why the names should be changed, and provides an account of destructive actions done by the person whom the bird is named after. The sole authority in officially naming and classifying North American birds is the American Ornithological Society, more specifically their North

American Classification Committee. More recently, the committee has held discussions on the mutually understood importance of changing bad bird names. There is an enormous amount of work to be done, and the process to systematically change common names will be difficult, but certainly worth it. So please keep the #BirdNamesForBirds conversation going. It is also worth noting that, for your personal birding expeditions, all names are useless and labels are low value. Feel free to rename whatever birds you wish, as long as the name does not cause harm.

HOW TO FIND BIRDS

Luckily for us, birds are found almost everywhere on the planet. They live on all seven continents, and there are even bird species that spend a significant portion of their lives flying over oceans, thousands of miles offshore. Finding a bird can be as simple as observing the birds right outside your window. But that's not to say birds are always easy to find.

Birding is like trying to collect all the special prizes from a cereal box. You never know what you'll find on a day of birding, and you're not guaranteed the bird you most covet, but you'll probably encounter some other really awesome species along the way. Birding can happen anywhere and at any time. Sure, parks exist, but have you watched birds in a parking lot? A lake has plenty of sights to offer, but have you watched birds in a retention pond behind a shopping center?

What is a cemetery but a park with extra architecture? Nature enthusiasts need not look further than their own home to enjoy the outdoors. Virtual birding is even an option. Livestreams can provide instant nature-watching from bird feeders, nests, and watering holes across the world at any time of day. And since nature is always action-packed and full of drama, nature cams are great shows to have on in the background while you do other things. They can definitely help pass the time on a slow day at work.

While there are no bad birds, some birds do get labeled "trash birds." Haters will call them rats with wings. Birds that can be found very readily and abundantly get the title of trash bird. The term *trash bird* can sometimes also be taken literally, with some such birds found unapologetically romping in the garbage. Trash birds shouldn't be deemed low in value, though, especially since the age-old adage "one person's trash is another person's treasure" holds true even in avian examples. Depending on your region, what you call a trash bird could be someone else's dream bird. Don't be discouraged from a deep appreciation for these species. Defend your regional trash bird mascot!

Birders are very adept at birding anywhere. When a birder tells you they "know a spot," be prepared to be taken to the back of an abandoned strip mall, a culvert on the side of the road, or the parking lot of an apartment complex to look for birds. Birds have successfully integrated into human-altered landscapes, and watching them in an urban context is just as exciting as watching them in rural areas. If you're really game, it may be worth a trip to the trash dump. An excursion to the local landfill will often reward those brave adventurers with rare bird encounters. The mounds of trash in a landfill would deter most reasonable people, but they are buffet tables for birds. Food scraps, insects, and rodents can attract a range of species. If birding at a dump isn't your style, other popular yet offbeat birding hot spots include cemeteries. (You can go one step further and protect birds by getting a conservation burial, an all-natural style of burial that also helps conserve land. Prairie Creek Conservation in Florida is a great example of a conservation cemetery. As an added bonus, Prairie Creek Conservation offers 2,000 acres of protected land to explore in this life and the afterlife.)

Depending on your level of participation, birding can involve long-distance trips to see a rare species. Rare bird alerts notify birders of uncommon species that have recently been reported in an area. Depending on the rarity, enthusiasts from every corner of the world may travel to the spot just for a chance to see or hear their target species. Ecotourism is one of the fastest-growing areas of the tourism economy, but it's not absolutely necessary to travel far and wide to see a bird. You can attract birds to your local patch with food and water. Better yet, fill the spaces near you with native flowers and shrubs. Birds can use the resources native plants provide year-round. The next rare bird that visits might be enticed to choose your yard as its new favorite spot.

Bird feeders come in a variety of styles that can meet your needs. Birdseed comes in a variety of mixes that target certain birds. Save yourself the stress by skipping the mixes with fillers and give the birds what they really want: sunflower seeds, peanuts, and suet. Suet is a mix of solidified fat gathered from beef kidneys. It can be combined with birdseed, cut into thick slices called suet cakes, and attached by string to a tree branch for a lucky bird—or even luckier squirrel—to snack on. However, the texture is far from that of a cake; instead it is a dense brick of greasy fat with the consistency of a peanut butter cup. This familiar confectionery consistency makes suet cakes the forbidden candy bar. Despite the ingredients list, a bold thought to take a small bite will forever linger in the minds of devoted birders.

Be sure to regularly sanitize your bird feeders, bird-baths, and suet cake holders to avoid spreading salmonella, finch eye disease, and other diseases to animals. Centralized feeding locations are potential disease spreaders if not maintained properly.

HOW TO BE A BIRDER

Modern-day birding takes on many different faces. Birding is becoming more diverse as birding activists push for inclusivity. The rules of birding are far less rigid than people outside of the hobby may perceive them to be. If you enjoy the sights, sounds, or vibes that birds provide, then you're a birder! There are no other requirements. These birds are for everyone.

Remembering so many bird names can be really difficult! Don't be afraid to make up names for the ones that give you trouble.

BIRDING TRADITIONS

Birding is full of traditions that make the hobby a party. Birding festivals are must-do events for any season. They're excellent places for birders to find new species and meet up with old and new friends. Festivals offer opportunities to get exposed to more birds through guided tours and workshops led by local birding experts. These events can be the glorification of a charismatic species, like the Yellow Rails and Rice Festival in southern Louisiana. They can also be jubilees of the season's special migrant visitors, like the Biggest Week in American Birding Festival in northwest Ohio. Whether local or abroad, festivals are a good excuse to take a few days off from the everyday routine and add some lifers to your checklist.

In birder lingo, a *lifer* is any species that you personally have yet to observe. Adding a lifer to your life list is a reason to celebrate! A life list is a compilation of all the species a birder has encountered. Life lists can be an actual list kept in a nature journal or a virtual one recorded in a birding app. A life list can also just be a mental checklist. Finding a lifer is such an exhilarating experience. The bird previously known to you only from references suddenly appears, but only for a few moments. Those few seconds move in slow motion as you try to make sense of the observation, while simultaneously being overwhelmed with satisfaction. In the moment of witnessing a lifer you may give way to a joyous dance. It's a justified reaction to a good bird encounter.

Birders celebrate adding a species to their life list by ending their day with a sweet treat. Eating *lifer pie* is the tradition of enjoying a slice of pie after adding a

 lifer to your list. When birders visit a new geographic area, they risk consuming lifer pie ad nauseam. If confections are not your preferred way to celebrate, you can also reward yourself in more visionary ways. Maybe doing lunges for lifers can give you that same endorphin rush others receive from a slice of pie. Lifer dances are also a way to celebrate, whether a choreographed dance with birding buddies or an unscripted boogie. There are approximately 2,000 species of birds in North America, which leaves approximately 2,000 pies, lunges, and dances to be had.

Lifers are not always easy to add. Given the seasonality of migrating species and the cryptic nature of

others, locating a must-find bird can lead birders on a wild goose chase . . . or maybe a snipe hunt. It can take some folks minutes to find a bird it has taken someone else years to document. No matter your skill level, a good portion of finding birds is just being lucky. Finding any species comes down to being in the right place at the right time. Just treat every bird as a gift.

In some instances, it can feel like your target bird species are particularly avoiding you and only you. It's hard to not take matters like this personally.

Bird species that repeatedly fail to reveal themselves are dubbed *nemesis birds*. But once you get proof of the little creature, you may find yourself overwhelmed by immense relief. You can sleep a little easier—that is, until the next time a bird evades your attempts to merely bless it with your humble discovery. These birds don't care about us. If they could offer some perspective on how birding makes them feel, I bet we would also be their nemeses.

Some birders use bird-watching apps to keep track of their observations. Some prefer more analog methods, like writing when and where they observed the first of a species on the respective pages within a field guide. Some birders don't keep track of the species they encounter at all. Competitive birders seek to record the most species for their observation check-lists. The most ambitious will dedicate a calendar year to find as many birds possible in the geographic area of their choosing. The yearlong campaign—called a Big Year—requires enormous effort. Big Year competitors are on the most extreme edges of the hobby and will push their limits to reach a goal. The 2011 comedy film *The Big Year* directed by David Frankel taps into this intensity. The film follows three birders competing to see the most species in North America; I can only imagine the local theatrics that have happened during city-, county-, and statewide Big Years.

Surprisingly, no one gets an award for doing the most in birding. What's the point of a competition where there aren't any prizes? Being dedicated enough to see "the most" of anything is pretty impressive. And we're on this spinning rock in the vacuum of space for only so long, so why not?

SELECTED BIRDS *of* NORTH AMERICA

ACORN WOODPECKER

Scientific Name: Melanerpes formicivorus

Habitat: Found in the western United States and throughout Mexico

The clownish appearance of Acorn Woodpeckers is just the beginning of the wacky life history of this bird. Acorn Woodpeckers hang out in family groups of a dozen or more. Generations of Acorn Woodpeckers live year-round in a communal tree. Their tree also serves as a food stockpile, called a granary, where they'll pull acorns as needed. Acorn Woodpeckers live in woodlands with multiple species of oaks, so they are not limited on acorn supplies. The granary consists of thousands of holes meticulously filled. Acorn Woodpeckers spend a lot of time tending to their wealth of acorns. They'll tap on each acorn in the granary to make sure it fits snugly into the tree hole, ensuring that it's not stolen by squirrels or other birds. Should an acorn come loose, the Woodpeckers will rehome the acorn to a more fitting hole.

In the breeding season, Acorn Woodpeckers have multiple breeding females lay eggs in one nest. The nest does not consist of typical material like twigs and lichen, but is instead formed from the wood chips that are created from excavating the tree cavity. These shavings act as a soft layer of nesting materials in the cavity. Acorn Woodpeckers have unorthodox nesting behaviors. Birds usually like to take care of young that are undoubtedly theirs. Since Acorn Woodpeckers nests communally, each breeding female will destroy the eggs of the other females before she begins laying. Once all breeding females begin laying, though, the massacre stops and incubation begins. Incubation and feeding duties are shared with the other members of the family circus.

AMERICAN KESTREL

Scientific Name: Falco sparverius

Habitat: Found throughout North America

The American Kestrel, formerly known as the Sparrow Hawk, is both the smallest and cutest falcon in North America. Their range spans nearly the entirety of the continent, and they can be found in a wide variety of open habitats. Kestrels can frequently be spotted during the day perched on utility poles and wires, surveilling grasses for a mouse, mole, or cricket to snack on. If the scanned area fails to arouse the tiny beast, they'll swoop over a few feet to the next utility pole and browse the new spot. If nearby perches are scarce, the Kestrel can hover over a field while searching for food. You can tell when a Kestrel has found prey because it will begin bobbing its head and wagging its tail. Eager to pounce upon its game, the Kestrel will then swoop from the air, land atop its prey, and pin it in its talons. Its sharp beak quickly gets to work.

Here's some dating advice from American Kestrels: feeding your significant other is a tried-and-true way to build trust. The backbone of every American Kestrel relationship is food. Male birds will offer females food items as part of their courtship display. If the male is successful in wooing, the pair will form a tightly bonded monogamous pair, remaining together year after year, in sickness and in health, to love and to cherish, until death do them part. So, step 1: meet for brunch; step 2: fall in love.

In the baby-making season, the pair will make a nest in a tree cavity excavated by other animals. Since many species of birds nest in cavities, Kestrel nests are sometimes shared concurrently with bird families of other species. American Kestrels have been reported successfully raising their young alongside the young of Bufflehead (*Bucephala albeola*) and Eastern Screech-Owls (*Megascops asio*).

AMERICAN ROBIN

Scientific Name: **Turdus migratorius**

Habitat: Found throughout North America

This familiar bird can be heard early in the morning, singing its conversational dawn song. They sound as if they are greeting the morning with a loud "*Chip! Cheerio! Cheery me!*" While American Robins share a name with and resemblance to European Robins—even using British-sounding greetings—they are not related to them. In fact, American Robins are not robins at all. They are related to thrushes, like the Wood Thrush (see page 143). Similar to Wood Thrushes, American Robins perform elaborate musical selections and prefer to forage lawns, fields, and gardens for worms. American Robins tilt their eyes toward the ground to get a better view of what's available to eat. When they spot something tasty, Robins will pounce, then jab the ground with their bills. They will use their strong legs to anchor to the ground while they dislodge worms stuck in the soil.

Female American Robins will build their cup nests in trees, but will also frequently settle on light fixtures and gutters for this construction project. While they still occupy the nest, young Robins are primarily fed earthworms. Now, you may have wondered how baby birds in the nest poop, and through our discussion of the Robin you are going to find out! Young Robins use the bird version of diapers, called fecal sacs, to stay tidy. Fecal sacs are membranous butt bubbles that contain baby bird excrement, wrapped up in a tiny package. While the baby bird pushes, the attending adult assists by pulling the fecal sac. Once the sac is free, the adult will eat it. Apparently, it's nutritious.

Every so often, the food sources of American Robins become scarcer in the northern parts of their ranges. The scarcity of resources can be due to the Robins themselves having been extremely prolific in previous breeding seasons. To avoid being at an awkward dinner party where there are too many birds and too little food, Robins will migrate farther south than is typical for their ranges. This astounding migration is called an irruption. On mornings during irruptions, American Robins will appear to explode from the treetops by the thousands all in search of a dinner party with better atmosphere.

AMERICAN WOODCOCK

Scientific Name: Scolopax minor

Habitat: Found in the eastern United States

These charismatic oddballs have gained a cultish following because of their unusual looks and interesting behaviors. American Woodcocks, also known as Timberdoodles or Bogsuckers, belong to the shorebird family Scolopacidae. Typically, you might imagine shorebirds as all those you see running behind receding waves on beaches as they look for a tasty bite. However, there are a considerable number of shorebirds that spend most of their lives in grasslands and even in the Arctic tundra, never to see a coastline in their lives.

American Woodcocks use their comically long, but highly sensitive beaks to probe moist soil in open fields or on forest floors for invertebrates, particularly earthworms. And their coloration reflects the places they most frequent as elemental colors help to mute their chunky shape among leaf litter.

At first glance, their body proportions appear slightly off, with ample eyes placed high and far back on a sizable head that is seemingly fused to a neckless plump body, not unliked a ping-pong glued to a football. Despite this clunky build, Woodcocks are surprisingly fluid in their movements. They frequently walk in a rocking motion that resembles a body isolation four-count. Pair a video of a Woodcock walking with any song and the Woodcock always stays on beat.

Woodcocks are crepuscular, meaning they are most active during dawn and dusk. The position of their doll-like eyes gives them panoramic vision behind and above, a great adaptation that helps them surveil predators and forage in low light. Evolution rearranged the rest of the Woodcock's head to make room for this strategic eye placement. Most birds have ears located behind their eyes, but Woodcocks have ears below their eyes. Evolution also shuffled some important brain parts for Woodcocks. Their cerebellum was relocated from the typical rear-brain position to the bottom of the brain.

In the breeding season, male Woodcocks put on a nightly theater show to attract females. Male Woodcocks will repeatedly belt out a nasally *peeeeent* that can be heard by humans up to 820 feet (250 m) away. A male will take flight from his peenting area and ascend, spiraling up to 300 feet (90 m) above the ground. Throughout his flight, the wind twitters between his feathers, emitting a series of rapid high-pitched whistles.

BALD EAGLE

Scientific Name: **Haliaeetus leucocephalus**

Habitat: Found throughout Canada, the United States, and northern Mexico

Bald Eagles, one of four eagle species to call North America home, are one of the most recognizable and culturally iconic species on the continent. However, Steller's Sea-Eagles (aka Pacific Sea-Eagles), White-tailed Eagles, and Golden Eagles are all slightly more majestic and grandiose than the better-known Bald Eagles. Although the Bald Eagle is without a doubt a beautiful bird, it has a few character flaws. Bald Eagles are secretly trash birds. Again, this is not a title meant to bring shame, but instead intended to draw attention to their trash-loving tendencies.

Bald Eagles can be found scavenging in dumpsters and landfills for some of their entrées. In 2020, the Cedar Hill Landfill in Seattle, Washington, was overwhelmed with Bald Eagles looking for a bite to eat. Hundreds could be found dining on trash at any given time. The amount of bird poop in such a concentrated area made working conditions difficult for landfill employees. The impact from this dumpster diving was felt miles away from the landfill as well. Bald Eagles would often take snacks to go and drop bits they didn't eat in people's yards. Lawns over a mile from the dump would have trash thrown all over them. However, due to the legal protections around Bald Eagles, Cedar Hill Landfill and the surrounding soiled residents had no other option but to grin and bear it.

Non-trash places where Bald Eagles are found include forested areas adjacent to rivers, lakes, and oceans. In these environments, Bald Eagles can be found scavenging carcasses and opportunistically stealing fish from other animals. They can snatch fish from Osprey (*Pandion haliaetus*) talons while in flight. Eagles will even bully anglers and offshore fishing boats for fish to steal. Bald Eagles truly don't make an honest living, but they sure do look amazing.

BAND-TAILED PIGEON

Scientific Name: Patagioenas fasciata

Habitat: Found in the western United States and throughout Mexico

Band-tailed Pigeons are the North American backcountry cousins of Rock Doves. The Band-tailed Pigeons' stocky shape, subtle coloration, and swift flight even lead them to closely resemble Rock Doves. This generalist species can be found from British Columbia to Argentina. They commonly live in alpine environments and can also be found in city parks, where flocks roam in search of nuts, berries, and seeds. Band-tailed Pigeon flocks can be recognized in flight by the clapping sounds of their wings.

Band-tailed Pigeons will feed their nestlings pigeon milk, a homemade nondairy milky substance created in the throats of both parents. The pigeon milk is made by special cells within the parent's crop, a muscular neck pouch that functions like a food pocket for birds. The milk is high in immune-boosting nutrients that help growing baby Pigeons become strong adults.

The same destructive past that led to the demise of Passenger Pigeons almost claimed Band-tailed Pigeons too. After years of overhunting, Passenger Pigeons were confirmed extinct when the last one died at the Cincinnati Zoo in 1914. Legal protections for Band-tailed Pigeons didn't come into effect until after public outrage from a massive slaughter of wild birds in 1912.

Ideas to resurrect Passenger Pigeons are being circulated in de-extinction research groups. Since Band-tailed Pigeons are the closest living relative to the Passenger Pigeon, the Band-tailed genome could potentially be used as the framework to revive this species of yesteryear.

BLUE JAY

Scientific Name: Cyanocitta cristata

Habitat: Found throughout the central and eastern United States and southern Canada

If you live around Blue Jays, then you are probably very familiar with their quirky behaviors. They are highly intelligent and highly social birds that make quite the ruckus. Notably, Blue Jays are able to produce an obnoxious variety of calls that generally have a metallic quality. They are also talented at mimicking calls of Red-shouldered and Red-tailed Hawks. In terms of personality, especially around feeding behaviors, Blue Jays are cafeteria bullies. When visiting a bird feeder, especially one with peanuts, Blue Jays may imitate a hawk to scare away other birds from the food. Once the competition ditches the buffet, Blue Jays can swoop in and hog the feeder.

Perhaps the most distinctive aspect of a Blue Jay is its brilliant color. But what goes into the color of a bird? Birds' feathers come to display the hue we see in one of two ways. Either the birds produce pigments or light refracts off the feather in a way to make a color appear. The blue coloration of any bird is not actually blue upon closer inspection. Blue is a structural color in bird feathers, visible only in the presence of light. If you hold up a Blue Jay feather in the light, it will appear blue. A Blue Jay feather held in the shade instead appears brown.

BLUETHROAT

Scientific Name: **Luscinia svecica**

Habitat: Found in Alaska

Bluethroats are found throughout Africa, Asia, and Europe; however, their North American range is limited to breeding populations on Alaskan tundras. Both male and female Bluethroats are talented mimics that readily copy the songs of neighboring songbirds. Males and females are similar in appearance, though the males will display bright blue neck feathers with inlaid black and orange patches. Female birds have lightly colored bibs with a necklace of dark streaks. During the breeding season, the blue feather bib on males becomes intensely blue. The ultraviolet reflectance of the males' throats is thought to play a role in mate selection, as female Bluethroats prefer to associate with males that have more reflective bibs. The bib has a series of concentric circles of brightly colored orange and blue feathers. The color patterns for these feather circles will vary by subspecies. The plumage in Alaskan males is reminiscent of a toddler with a spaghetti sauce and blue Kool-Aid–stained face. Despite the bright colors on males, this species can be hard to locate, as it slinks around thick bushes gleaning insects from branches and leaf litter on the ground.

BROWN PELICAN

Scientific Name: **Pelicanus occidentalis**

Habitat: Found on Pacific, Atlantic, and Gulf coasts throughout North America

What's a trip to the beach without seeing a squadron of Brown Pelicans harmoniously surfing the rolling waves? Or waking up from a sandy nap to notice that the private boardwalk across the beach supports a party of stoic Pelicans resting on dilapidated wood panels. When disturbed, they open their 78.7 inches (200 cm) of wings and delicately soar their broad build across the horizon. Experiences like these were almost lost during the mid-20th century. Brown Pelicans nearly went extinct in the 1950s due to widespread use of the pesticide DDT. The pesticide poisoned many species of birds, causing their eggshells to become thin and crack under the weight of an incubating adult. Brown Pelican populations plummeted since breeding adults in the 1960s and '70s could not successfully raise young. In 1972, DDT was banned in the United States and Canada, and its use was heavily restricted throughout Mexico in the 1990s. Populations of Brown Pelicans and other migratory birds affected by DDT didn't show recovery from the threats of extinction until the 1980s. However, Pelicans still face threats from oil production, fishing gear entanglement, and plastic pollution. Do what you can to help keep these beautiful behemoths here for everyone to enjoy.

Pelicans move with a surprising amount of grace given their large boat-shaped bodies, sinuous necks, and hefty bills. The gangly beasts can dive through 65 feet (20 m) of air at speeds around 40 mph (64 kph), catching fish swimming underwater with ease. How are Brown Pelicans able to survive such feats without shattering upon hitting the water? The Pelican's clunky design is the secret to surviving the impact from high diving. Right before contacting the water's surface, Pelicans take a deep breath that fills their air sacs and bones like a life vest. Pelicans will then jut their heads forward to pierce the water with their hydrodynamic bills, shooting their wings straight back to enter the water with as little resistance as possible, then extending their necks toward their prey underwater. Pelican's neck flaps open underwater like a parachute, grabbing food while also helping to soften the dive. The flaps, also called gular pouches, are the most famous feature of a Brown Pelican. Gular flaps are made of very strong yet stretchy skin supported by jawbones that can expand sideways. The pouches can hold 3 gallons (11 l) of water, which Pelicans must drain out of the sides of their mouths before swallowing their prey whole. The neck pouch is also helpful in regulating Pelicans' body heat. They will flutter their skin pouches to flow cool air across the blood vessels in their necks. Pelicans can be seen stretching their gular flaps over their necks, essentially turning their chin skin inside out in an unsettling event called glottis exposure. Pelicans may do this just because it feels nice to stretch their neck occasionally. It's putting in a lot of work!

Those are all the nice things about Brown Pelicans. But Pelicans have another troublemaking side seldom seen by beachgoers. How could something so refined also be one of the most menacing presences on shorelines? Because Brown Pelicans have a reputation of attempting to eat things they probably shouldn't. They've been caught unsuccessfully soliciting puppies, capybara, cats, and even humans to be their next meal. The tips of Brown Pelicans' bottomless pouches are hooked like a shepherd's staff, helping to funnel unsuspecting creatures into their gullets. They will try to eat anything that interests them. I'm not sharing this news to embarrass Pelicans, as they are not ashamed of raiding shorebird nest colonies to gobble up unsupervised young. I merely want to warn you not to leave your children or any small pets unattended around one. Although it is not the Pelicans' fault that they were awarded the tools to eat anything, they are not to be trusted.

CALIFORNIA CONDOR

Scientific Name: Gymnogyps californianus

Habitat: Found in the southwestern United States and northern Baja in Mexico

California Condors, previously known as Royal Vultures, are the largest and rarest birds in North America. Due to their size, they can have difficulty getting airborne. They may run downhill, with their gargantuan

9½ foot (3 m) wings spread in order to take flight. Once in the air, they can soar over ridges using air currents with their giant wings allowing them to stay aloft for hours.

California Condors are carrion eaters. They have featherless heads and necks, which allow them to enjoy a decomposing meal without getting their feathers dirty. Turkey Vultures, another common North American scavenger, similarly lack head feathers for this reason. The bare parts of California Condors can range in color from orange to pink, red, purple, and gray like a unique bruise.

California Condors are critically endangered due to lead poisoning and shooting. Lead pellets used to kill other animals would sicken scavengers that ate the carcasses. In the 1980s there were fewer than 30 wild California Condors. The last remaining birds were brought into captive breeding programs in 1987. After decades of captive breeding and habitat conservation the species is on the mend, however. As of 2021, the population of California Condors has reached 410. The U.S. Fish & Wildlife Service started reintroducing the birds into the wild in Southern California in 1992, and now the Yurok Tribe plans to restore California Condors to the skies of the Pacific Northwest after 100 years' absence. This enormous conservation feat could mean future generations are able to observe California Condors in their historic range. Folks who want their California Condor fix today can sit back and enjoy watching wild baby California Condors eat regurgitated decaying flesh live on 24-hour online nest cameras.

CAROLINA CHICKADEE

Scientific Name: Poecile carolinensis

Habitat: Found throughout the eastern United States

One of the few birds to be unanimously voted "cute" by all onlookers, these charming creatures live in wooded areas throughout the eastern United States. They can be spotted flipping and jumping along tree branches, much like feathered gymnasts, ridding leaves and bark of insects. Their songs are dulcet four-note tunes that sound as if they are saying "*Ca-ro-li-na*." They are highly curious, so don't be alarmed to find a Chickadee inquisitively watching you watching them.

In the northern part of their range, Carolina Chickadees overlap with their nearly identical cousins, Black-capped Chickadees. The two species likely separated from a common ancestor 2.5 mya, but that's not stopping the Chickadees from swapping genes today. Black-capped and Carolina Chickadees will hybridize where the populations overlap. To add to the confusion, the Chickadees can learn the one another's calls. So how can observers distinguish the two if the birds can mate with each other, learn each other's songs, and look nearly identical? Well, you can't! Trust me, it's easier to admit defeat than to try to learn their subtle differences. They're both supercute, so regardless of which species you may encounter, it's still a win.

DOVEKIE

Scientific Name: **Alle alle**

Habitat: Found in North Atlantic waters

This small, hearty auk is one of the most abundant seabirds in the world. Dovekies are gregarious colony birds and the North American equivalent to penguins, with a tuxedoed look and Arctic lifestyle. The

Dovekie's now extinct relative, the Great Auk, was considered the first penguin. By contrast, Dovekies are smaller descendants, standing approximately 9 inches (23 cm) in height, with small sparrowlike beaks. They are graceful while swimming in icy waters but clownish when moving on land. Their similarity to penguins is an excellent example of convergent evolution—the phenomenon where two unrelated species develop very similar life strategies and body shapes.

Unlike penguins, Dovekies can take to the skies with agility. Dovekies are skillful at evading animal predators, as living in a colony provides many pairs of eyes to search for potential dangers. When a threat is perceived, the Dovekie colony will take off in a swirling frenzy and remain reluctant to land. Dovekies' lack of speed on land, in addition to their unwary temperament toward humans, has made them a food source for people in Canada and Greenland. Dovekies breed near Greenland and travel to the western Atlantic near Quebec, Newfoundland, and New England. Dovekies can be spotted in large colonies called wrecks. Due to the Dovekie's northern range and seafaring life, it can be difficult for birders to experience them. Winter sea excursions off New England, though, may find Dovekies diving deep to eat zooplankton, crustaceans, and small fish from icy waters.

Most mating pairs are monogamous and reunite at the previous year's nest site to spend another breeding season together. Courtship displays involve a series of adorable bowing ceremonies, bill tapping, tandem walks, and preening. Their most awe-inspiring mating display involves slow, low flying. Dovekies make their nests in rocky crevices or on coastal cliffs where they lay one egg per year. The nests are lined with grasses and lichens for softness and small pebbles that prevent the delicate egg from rolling. Both parents will care for the egg and brood until the chick leaves the nest. Adult Dovekies will bring food back to their young using a specialized storage pouch in their neck. Neighboring nests will synchronize the time when chicks venture out to experience the ocean on their own, away from their parents. Radiating calls from fellow fledglings encourage other young birds to depart as a group. The chicks typically leave their nests late at night, between

9 p.m. and 2 a.m. Fledglings that fail to group up with other birds are highly susceptible to predation. A fledgling will also sometimes leave the colony with its male parent, who will care for it for about a month until the juvenile reaches independence.

Individuals not yet old enough to breed hang out in small groups called clubs.

ELEGANT TROGON

Scientific Name: Trogon elegans

Habitat: Found in southern Arizona and throughout western Mexico

Among the most beautiful birds to grace North America, the Elegant Trogon has a dedicated fan base. Elegant Trogons live year-round in a variety of habitats throughout Mexico, from tropical deciduous forests to semiarid thornscrub. Elegant Trogons are migratory in the northern extent of their range in Arizona. Southern Arizona has a reliable population of Elegant Trogons that spend their breeding season in high-elevation pine-oak forests along the cliffs of the Atascosas, Chiricahuas, Huachucas, and Santa Ritas. As the United States' most dependable location to see these emerald treasures, Arizona gets tens of thousands of birders visiting to observe Elegant Trogons annually.

Although their vivid colors and bulky build are reminiscent of parrots, Trogons are more closely related to owls. Like owls, Trogons' feet are configured in an *X* shape. This toe arrangement helps them hang vertically on trees. Elegant Trogons are cavity nesting birds, although they lack the ability to make a nesting cavity on their own. They recycle woodpecker nests after the woodpeckers leave the tree cavity.

Male Trogons engage in violent combat with each other for breeding territories and females to mate with. Females will also brawl to protect their nests, swooping down to peck and pummel intruders with their wings.

GAMBEL'S QUAIL, AKA SONORAN QUAIL

Scientific Name: Callipepla gambelii

Habitat: Found in the southwestern United States and northern Mexico

Gambel's Quail are charismatic Sonoran Desert denizens that live in brushy wildlands in addition to urbanized city complexes throughout their range. Their most characteristic feature is the bobbling bouclé that sprouts from their foreheads. Both males and females sport the fancy updo. Female Sonoran Quail have a blunt-cut topknot that peaks shortly above their brow line. Males have a more pronounced feather that looks like a ' kissed their heads. Out of all quail crests, this one deserves second place, being beat only by that of the Mountain Quail, which rises like an exclamation point atop their heads.

As a desert-dwelling species, the Sonoran Quail is adapted to handle the lack of water. They spend most of their time in river valleys and creeks that are lush in vegetation. Interestingly, these Quail do not need to drink water to stay hydrated. They can get all their required water from the food they eat. However, when a rare puddle forms in the desert, the Quail will still readily drink from it.

In the breeding season, Sonoran Quail will create ground nests tucked away under a prickly pear cactus (*Opuntia* spp.) or other brush. The female will lay around 10 eggs and incubate them for 23 days. As one of the desert's most sought-after morsels, Sonoran Quail can't risk slowly raising young in a nest the way altricial birds do. All the eggs in a nest will hatch within hours of one another. Once the whole gang is out, the parents and young will flee the nest. Sonoran Quail babies are ready to roam the world immediately after hatching and learn how to forage by closely watching mom and dad eat. Chicks will be cared for until they become independent, at around three months old. If their parents happen to die before the chicks are independent, other Sonoran Quail, including bachelor males, will readily adopt the abandoned young birds. It's pretty cute to watch dozens of fluffy Quail chicks follow their guardians around. These Sonoran Quail can also readily be found at backyard bird feeders. They are gluttons for milo.

Sonoran Quail like to mosey around their favorite snack spots in gregarious family groups at dawn and dusk. In the heat of the day, they loaf around in the shade and dust themselves in shallow ground baths to keep cool. When the bunch is threatened, they prefer to run away like track stars rather than take flight. They'll quickly find shelter under a cactus or in brush when disturbed.

GREAT BLACK-BACKED GULL

Scientific Name: Larus marinus

Habitat: Found along the Atlantic coast of North America

Gulls have a record of ruining beach cookouts by turning our meals into their meals. They are the city mouse's vulture, often found eating suspicious scraps of food left in streets, dumpsters, and parking lots in urban areas. Calling gulls trash birds is not inaccurate—they love the trash. But this is a habit that does the city a service and deserves more praise than it gets. Gulls are among the ranks of raccoons and opossums as misunderstood trash bandits. Gulls actually rate some respect. Plus, your real concerns should be focused on Brown Pelicans (see page 56). Gulls are cheeky and intelligent. Their ability to adapt to humans—and dare I say subdue them—should be applauded. Any bird that can learn how to trigger an automatic door, sneak into a snack aisle without the store owner noticing, grab a bag of chips, and walk back through the door with chips in tow wholly undetected deserves much more praise than persecution. Yes, that's something gulls have really learned to do.

On the surface, the gull family can be lackluster. Run through the gull section of a birding field guide and you will find photos of monochromatic birds that look and sound unnervingly similar. Observers are often left to piece together tiny details that distinguish one species from another. As if adult gulls were not enough of a headache to differentiate, younger gulls that have not reached full adult plumage can be even more difficult to identify. Juvenile gulls undergo yearly molts that change their feather patterns, and on top of that, similarly aged individuals of the same species can have variations in plumage patterns, and on *top* of that, gulls can hybridize. (If you disagree and think identifying gulls is simple, name three differences between Laughing Gulls and Franklin's Gulls—quickly. For the rest of us, it's understandable why people would lump them all together as, simply, *seagulls*.)

One gull that truly deserves to be identified, no matter what, is the Great Black-backed Gull. These birds are immense, wolfish eaters that live on the eastern coast of North America from Labrador to Florida. Their size, coloration, and pompous character lead them to resemble Bald Eagles. As one of the largest gulls in North America, it's understandable how they rose to the top of the food chain in their ecosystems. Great Black-backed Gulls are opportunistic eaters that will prey on mammals, fish, eggs, carrion, and other birds. They can develop a special appetite for shorebird hatchlings, tossing back chicks like popcorn.

GREATER PRAIRIE-CHICKEN

Scientific Name: Tympanuchus cupido

Habitat: Found in select portions of the central United States

This plump grouse had historical ranges that spanned the native grass prairies of North America from Canada through the central United States to Texas. Over the last 150 years, their range has become restricted to isolated patches in the central United States, primarily because of habitat loss. In appearance, males and females have similarly barred plumage patterns that help obscure them against grasslands. However, male Prairie-Chickens have a few bells and whistles that make them especially interesting to behold.

Greater Prairie-Chickens are famous for their "booming grounds" displays. The once common sights and sounds of Greater Prairie-Chickens performing their breeding displays are now a coveted interaction, rarely seen by observers. Like other birds, Greater Prairie-Chickens vocalize using their specialized voice box, or syrinx. Male Prairie-Chickens have special sacs on the sides of their neck that inflate to amplify their low-frequency booming sounds. To attract females, male Prairie-Chickens will congregate in open areas to perform. Their mating display consists of fluttering in the air, erecting their tails and ear tufts, producing their booming calls, and lots of stomping.

The existence of a Greater Prairie-Chicken implies the existence of a Lesser Prairie-Chicken. Lesser Prairie-Chickens are real birds found in very limited areas of Kansas, Oklahoma, New Mexico, and Texas. Despite their small stature, Lesser Prairie-Chickens are quite similar to Greater Prairie-Chickens.

GREEN JAY

Scientific Name: Cyanocorax yncas

Habitat: Found in southern Texas and eastern Mexico

The unmistakable bright green body and blue head of the Green Jay are sure to stop onlookers in their tracks when it first catches their eye. Its lovely coloration may even convert non-birders into believers. For those who don't get what all the hype around birds is about, it will all make sense when you spot your first Green Jay. If you thought North America only had Blue Jays, it will please you to know that there are many more kinds of jays—in all kinds of colors! It's hard to miss this flashy Jay as they are very vocal and hang out in family groups that consist of a breeding pair, their offspring from the previous year, and their offspring from the current year. The oldest offspring help defend territory, but are forced to find their own territories after the next group of youngsters leaves the nest.

Green Jays are nonmigratory and prefer open woodlands, citrus groves, and brush thickets dominated by mesquite trees. North American populations of Green Jays are restricted to a range from southern Texas down through eastern Mexico. They feed mostly on insects but will nibble on the occasional orange. In South Texas, they are commonly seen at backyard bird feeders eating seeds and yelling at nearby family members. During the hotter parts of the day, Green Jays can be found preening a family member in the shade.

HARLEQUIN DUCK

Scientific Name: Histrionicus histrionicus

Habitat: Found in northwestern North America, eastern Canada, and the coast of New England

The Harlequin Duck is a dazzlingly decorated bird that gets its name from the unique helmeted pattern of its head feathers. The X Games should make Harlequin Ducks an unofficial mascot since the compact

Duck lives an adrenaline junkie's dream. They can be found surfing cold, rapid, turbulent water along rocky shorelines from the Pacific coast of North America to the coasts of eastern Canada, Greenland, and New England. Their main food sources include crustaceans, barnacles, and invertebrates found in the rocky bottoms of white waters. The rockier the shore, the bigger the waves, and the choppier the water, the better as far as these birds are concerned. Harlequin Ducks would rather sleep on calm days, then break their bones on days when the already violent waters are especially brutal. That's not an exaggeration, either. These Ducks have been found with numerous broken bones, presumably caused by being repeatedly pummeled against rocks and frigid waves. They heal quickly, though—don't worry.

In the summer, Harlequin Ducks can be found in freshwater mountain streams. Their nests are laid next to rapidly moving waters, well hidden amid vegetation and rocks. In other seasons, the Ducks can be found out at sea. They migrate along the course of rivers rather than flying directly across terrestrial landscapes.

Maine is estimated to have over half of eastern North America's winter population of Harlequin Ducks. Large flotillas of lords and ladies can be seen chattering to each other. Note that Harlequin Ducks don't quack like most other ducks, instead they squeak like mice lost at sea.

HOODED WARBLER

Scientific Name: Tachycineta bicolor

Habitat: Found throughout North America

Hooded Warblers are arguably one of the easiest warblers to identify and one of the most striking to watch as they flitter among green leaves. They get their name from the black cap of feathers that frames their yellow

THIS IS A BOOK FOR PEOPLE WHO LOVE BIRDS

faces, almost as though the Hooded Warbler had a heavy-handed barber filling in its hair with spray-on dye. Males have more pronounced black caps and chin feathers that bluntly border their yellow body, while female Hooded Warblers have subtler hoods that blend into their yellow bodies.

Female Hooded Warblers weave their cup-shaped nests out of grasses and tree bark, situating them at the forks of shrubs. Their nests are sometimes the drop spot for Brown-headed Cowbird *(Molothrus ater)* and Shiny Cowbird *(Molothrus bonariensis)* eggs. Cowbirds are songbirds that have developed an evolutionarily genius reproduction strategy: instead of building nests of their own, they lay their eggs in other birds' nests and leave the parental duties to those birds. Hooded Warblers defend their territories against cowbirds. However, Hooded Warblers aren't equipped with cow-bird egg removal behaviors. If one successfully lays eggs in a Hooded Warbler's nest, the Warbler will fall for the trap, raising the cowbird eggs as its own.

Other warblers do have strategies to counter cow-bird nest parasitism. Yellow Warblers *(Tachycineta bicolor*) will thwart nest parasitism by rejecting the cowbird's eggs. Sometimes this means abandoning their own eggs or burying their eggs in a new layer of nest substrate. If a nest fails, Yellow Warblers will promptly build a new nest . . . right above the old nest. Should *that* nest fail, they'll build a new nest right above that one too. They'll just keep stacking until one of them works out. Maybe it's not an inventive strategy, but Yellow Warblers are just trying their best to get a successful clutch of youngsters out.

HOUSE SPARROW

Scientific Name: Passer domesticus

Habitat: Found throughout North America

House Sparrows are native to Eurasia and North Africa, but have been introduced to most continents outside of their natural range. House Sparrows are well established in North America and can be found in most places with houses—or any structure really. Their prevalence may lead them to be overlooked, though they're still worth observing if you know what to look for. House Sparrows are cavity nesters and will frequently build their homes in building crevices, traffic lights, and outdoor laundry vents. House Sparrows have even been found living 2,000 feet (610 m) below the ground in a coal mine.

In North America, House Sparrow numbers are declining at a rate of 3 percent per year. Although House Sparrows do take over cavity nests from native North American species, including woodpeckers, bluebirds, and Purple Martins, this decline is by no means a reason to celebrate. Even in their native range, House Sparrow populations have suddenly declined. European House Sparrow populations are down nearly 60 percent from their historic numbers. Reduced availability of nesting sites, food sources, and other resources is a big threat to common and specialized bird species alike.

LEWIS'S WOODPECKER, AKA FLY-CATCHING WOODPECKER

Scientific Name: Melanerpes lewis

Habitat: Found in southwestern Canada and the western United States

These are the most elaborately feathered of the wood-peckers of North America. They have shiny greenish-black heads and backs, red faces and bellies, and white necks. It's a shame that their name takes attention

---

away from the birds' beauty. Lewis's Woodpeckers are named after the early North American explorer Meriwether Lewis, of the Lewis and Clark Expedition. Outside of adventuring, Lewis also enslaved humans. Woodpeckers don't commit crimes against humanity and definitely deserve to be disassociated from the famed, and deeply problematic, explorer. Fly-catching Woodpecker is a much more fitting name, drawing on the interesting feeding behaviors of these majestic birds.

Unlike other woodpeckers, which bore into trees to find food, these Fly-catching Woodpeckers nab insects in acrobatic flight. They will sit on a perch to watch for insects. Once they spot something of interest, the Woodpeckers retrieve their prey and circle back to their perch. This feeding behavior is also common in the flycatcher family. In cooler months, when insects are less abundant, Fly-catching Woodpeckers will switch their diets to acorns and fruits. They will turn trees into pantries by storing extra acorns in holes they create. They can then take out food as needed.

LUCIFER HUMMINGBIRD, AKA LUCIFER SHEARTAIL

Scientific Name: Calothorax lucifer

Habitat: Found in West Texas, Southern Arizona, southern New Mexico, and throughout central Mexico

Although this bird enjoys living in hellishly hot conditions in the Chihuahuan Desert, Lucifer Hummingbirds are not eponyms for Satan himself. The word *lucifer* is Latin for "light bringing" and "morning star." It is a versed reference to the gaudy neck feathers on adult male Lucifers. During breeding displays, the gorget, or neck feathers, on male Lucifer Hummingbirds will fan out in the shape of a sun with rays. Unlike other hummingbirds, Lucifer Hummingbird females get to sit in their nests while males perform their elaborate mating display. A male's performance starts with him darting side to side while wagging his forked tail. The tail feathers clatter loudly as they rub against each other, like shuffling a deck of cards. He will then swiftly climb 100 feet (30 m) into the air before plunging back down at breakneck speeds to the nesting female. Female Lucifer Hummingbirds build nests made from cobwebs, blossoms, leaves, and lichens on ocotillo stems and agave stalks. Males don't help out with nest duties, so females will fiercely defend their nests and territories alone. Once the young leave the nest, they help the female defend patches of favorable shrubs and agave plants.

MASKED BOOBY

Scientific Name: Sula dactylatra

Habitat: Found in Hawaii and along the southern Atlantic and Gulf coasts

Masked Boobies are graceful seafaring birds that can be found roosting and breeding on small islands in tropical oceans. They have a patch of black feathers around their eyes that creates a masked effect. Other species of boobies, like the Red-footed Booby, have brightly colored feet, while the feet of Masked Boobies vary by subspecies and range from olive to gray, khaki, and even orange. Masked Boobies also have colorful faces that change hue depending on their age. Surprisingly, it is juvenile Masked Boobies that have the most colorful faces. They will have blue eye-rings, eyelids, and gular sacks until around two years of age, when they reach adulthood.

Masked Boobies are the largest species of booby and have a wingspan of around 63 inches (160 cm). They feed offshore, sometimes plunging 100 feet (30 m) through the air and into the ocean. Masked Boobies can often be found feeding near dolphins and tuna. The animals hunting underwater will push fish toward the surface, reducing the effort the Boobies need to exert to catch their prey.

During the breeding season male Masked Boobies try to impress females by bringing lucky ladies rocks and feathers. Paired Masked Boobies will create nests directly on the ground, along cliff edges, on their island homes. While incubating their eggs, adults will keep their backs to the sun. As the sun moves throughout the day, Masked Boobies follow it like a sundial. Because of this, by the time the eggs hatch, the nest will have an explosive ring of excrement around it. Female Masked Boobies will lay two eggs in their nests, but only one will hatch. The hatchling that emerges first will push its sibling out of the nest, leaving the remaining egg vulnerable to predators or a fall off the cliff face.

Boobies got their names when Spanish sailors encountered the birds and noticed their silly behavior and antics. The Spanish word *bobo*, meaning "fool or clown," was thrown around to describe the birds' featherbrained behavior of landing on sailing ships and being easily captured by sailors. Boobies likely thought the ships were a convenient place to stop for a moment. They would show no fear of humans and were extremely easy to catch. Time and time again, the boobies were oblivious to the consequences of alighting on the ships, which made them easy meals for the weary sailors.

MUSCOVY DUCK

Scientific Name: Cairina moschata

Habitat: Found wild along the Gulf Coast of Mexico, domestic populations throughout the United States

Wild Muscovy Ducks are found in wetlands and lowlands throughout coastal Mexico. They have large bodies, long necks, and sleek black feathers with green iridescence. Male Muscovy Ducks will have face warts, called caruncles, whereas females have smooth faces. Unlike other ducks, Muscovy Ducks don't quack. Their vocalizations are limited to hisses and grunts. Most of the wild Muscovy Duck's range can be found throughout Mexico, but some will reach South Texas and Florida. They can be seen moving in groups, foraging shorelines and calm waters for plants, invertebrates, and fish. Muscovies will poke their butts straight out of the water as they reach for food items farther below the surface.

If you are based in the United States, you might be familiar with Muscovy Ducks as the arrogant, multicolored, wart-faced ducks that people try to enjoy feeding in parks. Feeding feral Muscovy Ducks can be unpredictable, as the encounter depends on the temperament of the individual. Everyone knows someone who has been chased by an aggressive Muscovy Duck—don't let that someone be you.

Approach Muscovy Ducks with caution and be mindful generally when you are feeding waterfowl. If you do want to feed your local ducks and geese, please avoid giving them bread, as it is bad for their health and the health of their ecosystems. Instead, bring healthy snacks like peas, corn, and oats for the waterfowl to enjoy.

NORTHERN CARDINAL

Scientific Name: Cardinalis cardinalis

Habitat: Found throughout eastern North America

Northern Cardinals are the ruby-colored jewel of North America. Their loud calls pierce the air like laser beams. Listen closely to a Cardinal's call and you will hear the futuristic "*pew pew pew*" sounds shooting across the trees. Cardinals call and sing frequently to keep in contact with their lifelong mate—another bird that is often milling about a few feet away. The feather color of Cardinals, and most other birds with reds, oranges, and yellow feathers, derives from the keratin pigments in their food sources. Male Cardinals that eat high-quality red-colored berries become even more vibrant. Observing a male Cardinal in optimum feather condition will hypnotize observers into mindlessly uttering, "wow, that is a *really* red Cardinal." No matter how many times one sees a Cardinal, a *really* red Cardinal will always elicit such a response. Female and juvenile Cardinals have more warm-brown feathers on their bodies and red-tinged wings and tails. Female Cardinals, like male Cardinals, are studded with the perfect tool for a seed-eating bird—a chunky, orange, triangular beak that comes to an intimidating point.

Cardinals' red hue also signals their fiery temperaments. At the bird feeder, Cardinals mean business and will take little from other foraging birds. The crimson birds are seed defenders that meet adversaries with a confrontational open beak. Scientists that use mist nets to capture and study birds unanimously agree that Cardinals are intimidatingly fierce. A Cardinal will latch on to any wayward digits and draw blood without question, even if those hands are gathering data that helps create conservation strategies for birds and their habitats. Perhaps we might say that Cardinals are stained with the blood of their enemies?

Canada and the western United States are mostly devoid of Northern Cardinals. Mexico and the eastern United States boast Northern Cardinal populations so prolific, some people may consider Cardinals trash birds. However, we can certainly count on all southern grandparents to appreciate every single Redbird they come across. After all, how often does one find a bird *so* red? Northern Cardinals are nonmigratory and prefer brushy habitats interspersed with open areas. Once they've found an area, they'll often stay put and establish home ranges. It's possible that the Northern Cardinals that frequent your area have had that established home range for years. A lineage of Cardinals and their royally red descendants may have long occupied the space that now supports your homestead.

Only two species of cardinals live in North America. *Cardinalis cardinalis*, highlighted here, and *Cardinalis sinuatus*, commonly known as Pyrrhuloxia. Northern Cardinals are the ruby-studded lead singers of the cardinal family, whereas Pyrrhuloxias are the aging bros that use too much gel on their thinning top crest. Pyrrhuloxias are considerably drabber that their ruby brethren, sporting gray feathers on the body with red accents on the wings, chest, face, and crest. Female Northern Cardinals and Pyrrhuloxias can be confused for each other, but the round gray-yellow beak of the Pyrrhuloxia is a key feature that sets them apart from their Redbird cousins.

NORTHERN JACANA

Scientific Name: Jacana spinosa

Habitat: Found along the Gulf and Pacific coasts of Mexico

The Northern Jacana is a year-round resident of wetlands found along the shores of Mexico. The exceptional physique of Jacanas is worth admiration. While the Northern Jacana is yet another bird that appears as if it were put together with spare prehistoric parts, it is also a species that looks comfortable in its awkwardness. Northern Jacanas' scientific name pays homage to the spiny growths they have hidden on the inside of their wings, bright yellow spurs they use to fight with one another. Their more conspicuous feet deserve attention as well. Northern Jacanas have greatly elongated toes and nails. Their large feet evolved to allow them to walk effortlessly across lily pads and algae floating on the water. With the leading step, Jacanas ease their weight across their spread toes. The trailing step moves with toes together, then swings forward to reopen the toes and bear the bird's weight. Northern Jacanas are also known as the Jesus Bird, because of their ability to practically walk on water.

Northern Jacanas have a polyandrous mating system, in which female Jacanas seek out multiple male partners. Male Jacanas will establish territories and be visited by females. Females may find up to four males to partner up with. In each territory, the dominant female will actively push out any other females that may try to enter. Should another female Northern

Jacana make advances on an already claimed male, he will do everything in his power to make her go away. The male Jacana will even call out to his mate to come take care of the stranger in their marsh. A female Jacana will lay eggs in separate nests for each of the males she has chosen and leave parental care to them. Each male takes over all incubation and rearing duties, and even makes the nest for his partner to lay her eggs in.

Jacana young are precocial, meaning they are ready to roam the world and feed on their own shortly after hatching. The young are covered in fuzzy down feathers and stand on preposterously long legs that put runway models to shame. The young can be found swimming across areas where the water is too deep. When the young need to escape aerial predators, they will dive into the water, leaving only their beaks above the surface to act as snorkels.

NORTHERN MOCKINGBIRD

Scientific Name: Mimus polyglottos

Habitat: Found in southern Canada and throughout the United States and Mexico

Although Northern Mockingbirds hardly need any introduction, I will do my best. The all-time champ of copying hundreds of sounds, undefeated in swooping at anything too close to their nests, the mimic that always makes birders stop and listen twice, and definitely one of the species on your home list—I proudly present the Northern Mockingbird. Northern Mockingbirds have an expansive range throughout Mexico and the United States. They are a generalist species found in a variety of habitats, from suburban lawns to deserts. Their scientific name translates to "many-tongued mimic," in reference to their impeccable impersonations.

Both male and female Mockingbirds sing. The fittest males sing during the day to find love. Less impressive males can't compete and must sing during a quieter time when they are less likely to be drowned out by other sounds. Nighttime is when the lonely and especially desperate males shine. Unfortunately, they sing of an unrequited love. The lonely males certainly do attract the attention of disgruntled human neighbors trying to sleep, though.

Young Mockingbirds are especially receptive to learning songs. They eavesdrop on adults' songs, commit them to memory, then practice what they learned as best they can. At 1–2 months old, juvenile

Mockingbirds begin to quietly sing. Mockingbirds remain students of song throughout their lives. They will add newly learned songs to their repertoire as needed. Mockingbirds are not able to reproduce every sound there is. Some sounds, like trills, are too complex even for this masterful mimic.

THIS IS A BOOK FOR PEOPLE WHO LOVE BIRDS

OSPREY

Scientific Name: *Pandion haliaetus*

Habitat: Found throughout North America

Meat-eating birds are too cool for words. Ospreys are found on every continent except Antarctica and require open bodies of water to catch fish as their main food source. Due to their pescatarian habits, Ospreys are often called Fish Hawks or Fish Eagles. However, Ospreys are neither hawks nor eagles. Ospreys are in a classification all their own. They are the sole representatives of the Pandionidae family.

Ospreys are exceptional water hunters, physically adapted to catch fish. With their keen eyesight Ospreys can spot fish below them while flying 130 feet (40 m) in the air. They wait patiently for the perfect moment to dive at their target, and their accuracy is unaffected by any reflections on the water's surface. Ospreys dive into water talons first, with feet opened wide and slightly overlapping, to essentially create a fishing net with hooks. Their extremely long talons latch on to the fish with a vice grip. Ospreys only dive about 3 feet (1 m) into the water to catch fish. Extremely powerful wings then lift Osprey and prey back out. The captured prey can weigh 10–50 percent of the Osprey's mass. Should an Osprey grasp a fish too large for it to fly off with, the bird risks drowning.

Once back in the air, Ospreys can maneuver its catch to a front-facing position for a more aerodynamic flight. As they carry their prizes off toward a safe perch to eat, Ospreys can often be heard giving out a victory screech.

Ospreys create massive nests made of sticks at the tops of tall trees or on human-made nest platforms. Their nests can become large enough for an adult human to theoretically sit on it. Other birds like European Starlings and House Sparrows may even sublet small sections of the Osprey's nest to build their own nests. The Osprey family upstairs doesn't seem to mind at all.

PAINTED BUNTING

Scientific Name: **Passerina ciris**

Habitat: Found in the southern United States and throughout Mexico

The beauty of the Painted Bunting makes it seem like a bird that belongs in a tropical climate with other unbelievably colorful birds. However, the artistry of Painted Buntings is very accessible to fans throughout their

North American range. Painted Buntings can be found on the ground foraging in grasses and low shrubs.

Only adult male Painted Buntings display the vivid colors. Females and juvenile males are entirely and marvelously shades of vibrant green. Males can easily be spotted singing in treetops in the spring and summer. Since only male Painted Buntings are reported to sing, an easy way to distinguish adult females from juvenile males is to observe this behavior. The expressive ramblings of males defending territories can be heard throughout grasslands with scattered brush and trees. In the winter, Painted Buntings migrate to Mexico and return to the same territory they have defended in previous years. Next time you visit a restaurant that offers crayons to kids, impress your table guests by using the four basic colors you're given to draw a Painted Bunting.

PLAIN CHACHALACA

Scientific Name: Ortalis vetula

Habitat: Found in southern Texas and along the Gulf Coast of Mexico

The Plain Chachalaca is a relative of chickens, and an adventurous one at that. This species of bird likes to climb trees and venture out onto perilously thin branches. Chachalacas have a distinctive sound and can be heard calling out "*Cha-cha-la-ca*" from treetops. Choruses of Chachalacas will scream together in ear-splitting pandemonium. The valleys that surround their typical ranges will ring out with the birds' chaotic sounds. Due to this habit, Plain Chachalacas are usually heard before they are seen. Their vocalizations and forage outings are concentrated in the cooler parts of the day. They will consume fruits, seeds, and leaves while sitting in a tree with other Plain Chachalacas. In the afternoons, they will lie flat on the ground with wings outstretched to sunbathe. At dusk, family groups will roost together, huddled along a selected branch and leaving no space between one another.

ROCK DOVE

Scientific Name: Columba livia

Habitat: Found throughout North America

Rock Doves are the reigning royalty of trash birds. They are more commonly known as Pigeons—the same birds fed by well-meaning folks on park benches every-where. However, since there are about 36 different

THIS IS A BOOK FOR PEOPLE WHO LOVE BIRDS

species of pigeons in the *Columba* genus, simply calling these commonplace birds Pigeons is discouraged. But calling them Rock Doves or Rock Pigeons is acceptable, since many of the *Columba* pigeons use *Dove* interchangeably in their common names.

Rock Doves were introduced to North America in the 17th century by colonizers on the Atlantic coast and can now be found nationwide in the United States, particularly in urbanized areas. Wild Rock Doves are native to Europe, North Africa, and southwestern Asia, but feral colonies have readily expanded, dramatically increasing cosmopolitan distribution. Can you even recall the last time you were in a city and didn't encounter a Rock Pigeon? Their abundance is partially thanks to the endless heaps of trash humans produce, which then nourish little baby Rock Pigeons, and infrastructure like tall buildings and highway overpasses, which support their nests.

Rock Pigeons come in an array of colors and feather types. The ones encountered in city centers may have white, coppery-brown, and near-black appearances. Domestic Rock Pigeons are bred for their outward characteristics, similar to pedigreed dogs. There are over 800 breeds of domestic Rock Pigeons, which leaves plenty of room for some to look absolutely ridiculous (see the Berlin Short-faced Tumbler).

Rock Pigeons are so prolific that they will (hopefully) never be eradicated—although, another once common dove species, the Passenger Pigeon, that once flocked in hoards so numerous they would block out the sun as they flew overhead is now gone. And even more notably, the Dodo—yes, the famous flightless bird—was also a species of pigeon that met an unfortunate demise at the hands of humans.

ROCK PTARMIGAN

Scientific Name: **Lagopus muta**

Habitat: Found on the coasts of Greenland and throughout northern Canada and Alaska

Rock Ptarmigan are stocky chicken-like birds that live throughout the Arctic. They rely on sparsely vegetated alpine and Arctic tundra with plenty of rocks, as their name implies.

Both males and females don nearly all-white plumage in winter to better conceal themselves in the snow. Every night, Rock Ptarmigan will tuck themselves into the snow to sleep. When it's bedtime, they bulldoze their way through layers of snow to create a cave. In shoddy weather, Ptarmigan may spend the whole day under the snow. Their snowy sleeping chamber is actually well-insulated and helps keep them cozy. Their natural snow gear is exceptionally good at protecting the birds while they sit under layers of snow. The lower half of their body feathers come equipped with extra heat-trapping layers to keep the birds warm through the frigid Arctic winter. As winter approaches, their feet grow more feathers and longer claws, essentially becoming snowshoes, to better allow the birds to walk across the tundra.

Their summer plumage is much more elemental, which helps Ptarmigan disguise themselves as rocks. Male Rock Ptarmigan are slow to take on their summer camouflage and will retain their frosted look to attract mates. In their breeding display, males will raise their clownish crimson eyebrows, extend their necks, fan out a single wing, and waltz around any open-minded female Rock Ptarmigan. After their nuptials, males will purposefully dirty their alabaster plumage to become less conspicuous. (Step 1: Make babies. Step 2: Stay alive.) To create a nest, females will scrape shallow depressions in the dirt then line the bowls with their own feathers. Female Rock Ptarmigan use their mottled feathers to conceal the nest against the rocky terrain.

ROSEATE SPOONBILL

Scientific Name: *Platalea ajaja*

Habitat: Found along the Gulf Coast shoreline of North America and the Pacific coast of Mexico

When admired from a distance, Roseate Spoonbills appear to be graceful waterbirds. Upon closer inspection, Spoonbills are actually quite bizarre to behold. Roseate Spoonbills can look as if they have taken fashion advice from prehistoric birds and never thought to update their look. Their leading feature is, of course, that namesake bill, which becomes rough in texture as the Spoonbill ages. A yellow-orange neck pouch marries their bills to their elongated necks. Roseate Spoonbills' partly bald heads leave their disc-shaped ears exposed, while their bloodred eyes stand in contrast to their color-changing faces. Their football-shaped bodies are supported by long, thick legs, even thicker knees, and elongated toes. Still, this strange combination of parts makes Roseate Spoonbills all the more appealing.

Roseate Spoonbills are usually found wading in shallow coastal marshes, swamps, mangrove forests, and mudflats. They spend their day sweeping their appropriately named bills side to side, with mouths slightly agape, in search of food. When their bills bump into something of interest—namely minnows, insects, plant bits, and crustaceans—Roseate Spoonbills will scoop up the item. Similar to flamingos, Roseate Spoonbills' pink color is derived from the food they eat, albeit secondhand. The crustaceans in their diet eat algae containing pink and red pigments. When Roseate Spoonbills consume the crustaceans, the carotenoid pigments from the algae are expressed outwardly in their feather color.

In the breeding season, their featherless heads will turn a distinctive yellow-green, and their feathers will become profoundly pink, as if painted with over-the-counter nausea, heartburn, and indigestion medicine. Roseate Spoonbills are colony nesting birds. They can be found nesting with egrets, cormorants, herons, and ibises on small islands not far from shore. Sometimes, the entire nesting colony will fly up and circle the area for no apparent reason.

SANDHILL CRANE

Scientific Name: Antigone canadensis

Habitat: Found throughout Canada, the central and eastern United States, and northern Mexico

Sandhills are towering, large-bodied, long-necked birds known for migrating in huge flocks across the continent. Sandhill Cranes are very noisy and will announce their arrivals and departures with fanfare.

Their trumpetlike calls are produced from the syrinx and amplified by their long tracheas. As one of the most celebrated cranes, Sandhill Cranes have captivated people's attention throughout their range. Spectators look forward to their respective Sandhill Crane seasons and even hold festivals dedicated to their local arrival.

Sandhill Cranes are separated into distinctive populations, which follow generally defined migration routes. The breeding and wintering grounds of Sandhill Cranes depend on which population they belong to. During their migrations, Sandhill Cranes will stop over at various locations along the long journey to grab a meal and rest. They will opportunistically eat plant matter, invertebrates, and small vertebrates found in shallow grassy wetlands. Leftover grains in harvested agricultural fields are major sources of food for the Atlantic Flyway population.

Sandhill Cranes have some impressive moves in times of love and war. They have very adorable courtship displays that involve dancing, stick tossing, pumping their heads, and stretching their wings upright.

When the Cranes need to be combative, they will fly toward the threat while kicking their feet and thrusting their bills in a stabbing motion at the troublemaker.

SHORT-TAILED ALBATROSS

Scientific Name: Phoebastria albatrus

Habitat: Found in the northern Pacific Ocean

The Short-tailed Albatross was once a common sight along the western Pacific Ocean. Unfortunately, the species is now vulnerable to extinction due to over-hunting and plumage collection. It is estimated that around 1,200 Short-tailed Albatrosses exist today, and of that population only half are breeding adults. They have a very limited North American range and can be commonly encountered off the coasts of Alaska. Signs of hope have shown up in Hawaii, where nesting pairs of Short-tailed Albatrosses have recently been found.

Albatrosses are long-lived birds. The oldest known living wild bird is a female Laysan Albatross named Wisdom. Wisdom was first banded by scientists in 1956, when they estimated she was already five. As of 2021, Wisdom is at least 70 years old.

SNOWY OWL

Scientific Name: Bubo scandiacus

Habitat: Found throughout Canada, Alaska, and the northern United States

Despite their mysterious allure, Snowy Owls can frequently be seen spending their winters in cities along the U.S.–Canadian border. Due to the added structures characteristic of human-altered landscapes, like skyscrapers and power lines, city-dwelling Snowy Owls will be more frequently seen on light poles, building ledges, and fence posts during the winter. However, in the summer this species of owl spends most of its time sitting on the ground. The Arctic tundra doesn't exactly have trees, so what can you expect from Snowy Owls?

Snowy Owls rely on their keen senses to help them scan the landscape for prey. Their eyesight allows them to pick up movement from about a mile (1.6 km) away, and their hearing can detect movement under almost 8 inches (20 cm) of snow. Their main food source is lemmings, the goofy little rodents that follow each other. During a single year, Snowy Owls can eat around 1,600 lemmings. How do they do it? Snowy Owls are able to use their ground nests like mini refrigerators. Male Snowy Owls will bring freshly captured food to their partners and nestlings, and female Snowy Owls will then stash the extra lemmings in their nests. The layers of cached lemmings can make the nests look like they were built from fur coats. When the nest fridge is full, female Snowy Owls will store extra food items in a second pile, away from the nest. The fridges stay stocked so their nestlings can always have a bite to eat. In years when lemmings are abundant, Snowy Owls can raise double or triple the number of young compared to low lemming years.

Snowy Owls have been appreciated for millennia. Renderings dating back 17,000 years have been found in caves, drawn by prehistoric people who knew how to appreciate a good bird.

TREE SWALLOW

Scientific Name: *Tachycineta bicolor*

Habitat: Found throughout North America

This holographic member of the swallow family surprisingly does not frequent trees outside of the nesting season. The rest of the year, Tree Swallows frequent open fields to chase insects in a series of acrobatic tumbles that showcase their greenish-blue iridescent feathers. Compared to other swallows, Tree Swallows have unique diets as they can eat seeds and berries along with insects. During breeding months, they can be found eating old eggshells, clamshells, and fish bones for an added boost of calcium that will benefit their forthcoming nests. If you live in their territory, you may find a Tree Swallow rummaging through your compost pile in search of calcium-rich food bits.

Tree Swallows are highly social, especially during the winter. In winter months, they can be found migrating with thousands of their kind en route to Mexico. Around sunset, in a spectacular display of agility and synchrony, thousands of Tree Swallows will create a massive swirling vortex to funnel into their nighttime roosts among the reeds.

TUFTED PUFFIN

Scientific Name: *Fratercula cirrhata*

Habitat: Found in the Pacific Ocean

Tufted Puffins can easily be described as handsome. Their chiseled beaks, steely eyes, and coif feathers make these seafaring birds stand out. The contrasts between their orange bills, white masks, golden head plumes, and black bodies demand everyone's attention. Tufted Puffins keep up this vibrant display during the breeding season. Otherwise, they sport an all-black body with a pale yellow bill.

About three million Tufted Puffins, which account for nearly 80 percent of all Tufted Puffins, breed in North America. In summer months they will build nests on small islands off the Pacific coast from Alaska to Northern California. They'll be found hopping, walking, and clinging to rocky cliffs. Their nests are settled 5 feet (1.5 m) deep, earthbound in cliffside holes. A sole egg is cared for by both parents. In the winter, Tufted Puffins can be found far away from land, surfing the north-central Pacific Ocean for invertebrates and fish.

Tufted Puffins are awkward fliers. They can't take flight directly from the ground, so instead they throw themselves from cliffs to get airborne. Once in the air, they are rigid but powerful aviators capable of nimbly gliding to the waters below. Right before hitting the surface, Tufted Puffins tuck into a splashless dive. Their swimming abilities closely resemble flight. They will flap their wings to propel themselves through the water to proficiently catch schools of fish. Their bills have grooves that allow them to hold more than a dozen small fish at one time. To fly back to shore, Tufted Puffins need a long running start. They will walk on water while flapping their wings to gain the momentum for takeoff. Landing on solid ground also proves very difficult for Tufted Puffins. The best they can do is come in for a crash landing.

WHITE IBIS

Scientific Name: *Eudocimus albus*

Habitat: Found along the Gulf and Pacific coasts of Mexico

The most striking features of the White Ibis are, of course, its nearly all-white body sandwiched between bright red legs and head. That essentially summarizes the whole bird—simple in design but very elegant all around. The strikingly red bare parts get their coloration from the birds' diet, comprised largely of red crustaceans.

Historically, the White Ibis is one of North America's most abundant wading birds. If you've ever found yourself in Florida, you can likely attest to this from witnessing hordes of White Ibises throughout streets and front yards. They are quite habituated to living close to humans. Congregations of White Ibises will creep across yards, probing the ground for insects. If they are not exterminating bugs in lawns, they may be found in shallow wetlands, sweeping for crawfish, crabs, frogs, and snails. The massive bills resembling barbecue tongs on their faces may initially seem ill-adapted to maneuver struggling prey into their mouths. However, White Ibises can skillfully lift and lower squirming morsels in their stiff beaks before sending food down the hatch.

Like other highly social birds, White Ibises spend nearly all their time with wading birds of a feather. Finding protection in numbers, groups of White Ibises will seek out a common tree to roost in for the night. White

Ibises will also nest in large colonies, numbering up to thousands of individuals. Male White Ibises will form parties of bachelors that will display together to attract the attention of desirable females. A group of displaying males is a spectacle to behold. Their ritual courtship behaviors include chewing on twigs, bathing, and group flights in which thousands of bachelors swirl up and down. Females may accept a male's advances by sharing a twig that they can shake together. The pair will continue to greet each other with twigs to further strengthen their bond. (These birds love twigs.) When it comes time to construct their nests, White Ibises will seek out the finest of twigs and steal a couple of the really good twigs from neighboring Ibises' nests.

WOOD THRUSH

Scientific Name: Hylocichla mustelina

Habitat: Found throughout the eastern United States and the Gulf Coast of Mexico

Wood Thrushes are neotropical migrants that spend their winters in Mexico then fly to the eastern United States to spend their summers. Wood Thrush migration routes require the birds to fly across the Gulf of

---

Mexico. In preparation for one of the most arduous flights they will take, Wood Thrushes will chow down on high-energy berries in order to pack on fat reserves they can use during the nonstop flight. Wood Thrushes will also forage in leaf litter, searching for invertebrates to eat. They can be found hopping on the ground and scraping the forest floor with their long legs.

Have you heard the sound of a Wood Thrush? Their songs are arguably one of the most melodic bird tunes to fill eastern U.S. woodlands in the summer. They are often the first birds to begin the morning chorus and the last birds to sign off for the night. Wood Thrushes take the stage on leafless limbs of tall trees and resonate airy, flutelike notes that instantly enchant the forest. The melodies rain down from the midstory and cover the woodland with harmonies. Because of the unique anatomy of bird voice boxes, Wood Thrushes can sing multiple notes at the same time to produce chords that rival the musical prowess of The Clark Sisters.

ZONE-TAILED HAWK

Scientific Name: Buteo albonotatus

Habitat: Found in the southern United States and throughout Mexico

If it looks like a vulture, flies like a vulture, and hangs out with vultures, it just might be a Zone-tailed Hawk. (Consider this a reminder that birders need to stay diligent and check for the hidden gems that occasionally

---

hide in a large flock of commonly seen birds.) Zone-tailed Hawks bear a striking resemblance to Turkey Vultures, an underappreciated scavenger with a widespread North American range. This aesthetic similarity may be a tactic to trick squirrels, lizards, and smaller birds into thinking the predator is harmless to them. But the similarity could also just be a coincidence. Farther south in their range, Zone-tailed Hawks also resemble another species: the Common Black Hawk.

Like many hawks, Zone-tailed Hawks have extremely acrobatic courtship displays. Their sky dances involve the breeding pair dipping, rolling, and looping 980–1,640 feet (300–500 m) in the air. After reaching their maximum altitude, the pair begins to sway around each other, forming figure eights in the sky. Some may also lock talons and spiral headfirst toward the ground as part of their hour-long mating display.